THE PICTORIAL HISTORY OF

TRIUMPH

MOTOR CYCLES

IVOR DAVIES

CHANCELLOR
PRESS

First published in Great Britain in 1985 by
Temple Press

This edition published in 1996 by
Chancellor Press
an imprint of Reed Consumer Books Limited
Michelin House, 81 Fulham Road, London SW3 6RB
and Auckland, Melbourne, Singapore and Toronto

ISBN 1 85152 906 3

Printed by Bath Press, Avon

Jacket picture acknowledgements:
Front jacket / back jacket detail;
The National Motor Museum, Beaulieu

Contents

Introduction

In this book I have endeavoured to present a chronological collection of photographs from the early days of Triumph to the more recent past. Triumph goes back a long way, 100 years in fact, and it is a happy coincidence that this book should be published during the 100th anniversary of the founding of the company.

Inevitably some of the early photographs have been seen before because photography was not so prolific in those days as it is today, and in consequence the number of surviving photographs is strictly limited. Fortunately things had improved when I came on the scene and it was my practice as Triumph Publicity Manager to record on film every development, whether it was a new seat, a cylinder head or a complete machine. These pictures often came in useful later when the engineers had forgotten where they had located that drain plug on a long-scrapped prototype. They were also used as a basis for illustrations in the many and varied items of sales and service literature that we produced. There are gaps in the chronological sequence where suitable photographs could not be found but most of the gaps have been filled by photographing catalogue pages and I am deeply indebted to my son John for his painstaking efforts with these period pictures which show what can be done with a modern camera even if the original half-tone illustrations are anything up to eighty years old.

Each picture has a fairly lengthy description with historical and technical details where these are relevant. This, I hope, will appeal to the reader who has a genuine interest in the subject and who wants more information than the usual "1925 550cc Triumph" type of caption supplies. Triumph has an interesting history and as it has appeared in one form or another in virtually every book that has been written about Triumph, I have arranged things a little differently here. The photographs are divided up into five convenient periods of years and each period has an introduction in the form of a brief historical resumé of the significant happenings in that period. The reader can then relate this directly to the photographs that follow. Now, as the company existed for seventeen years before producing its first motor cycle and to include this would make the introduction to Chapter One too long and complicated, here is the story of those early days.

The founder was a young and impecunious German named Siegfried Bettmann who came to England in 1883 from his home in Nuremberg. After working briefly as a foreign correspondent and overseas representative in London, Bettmann set up his own company, S Bettmann & Co., in 1885 to sell bicycles abroad. This was at the time of the great cycle boom and he could see good business opportunities in this exciting new form of personal transport. He bought his bicycles in Birmingham and gave them a "Bettmann" label but soon realised that this name was not entirely acceptable for a British product so he hit on the name "TRIUMPH" in 1886, reckoning that this would be readily understood in most European languages. In 1887 the name of the company was changed to The Triumph Cycle Company.

At this point Bettmann was joined by Mauritz Schulte, engineer, and a fellow countryman from Nuremberg. It had always been the intention to manufacture rather than factor bicycles and now with a first class engineer as partner, a small factory was rented in Much Park Street, Coventry. From this grew the extensive business which made the name Triumph world famous. Coventry at that time was the centre of the cycle trade and went on to become celebrated for its motor cycles, cars, aircraft, aircraft engines, machine tools and many other engineering products.

Came the turn of the century and bicycles fitted with the new fangled petrol engine began to "phut-phut" an erratic path along the roads of Coventry and elsewhere. Schulte became intensely interested in this new development, seeing it as a possible replacement for the bicycle. After much experiment he produced in 1902 the first Triumph motor cycle. This was a suitably modified bicycle fitted with the best engine then available, the 2¼ hp Minerva from Belgium. By 1905, Triumph were making their own engines and this practice continued to the present day.

Schulte's high standards soon established an unrivalled reputation for quality and reliability at a time when such virtues were in very short supply in the motor cycle industry. *Ixion* (Canon B H Davies), that famous contributor to *The Motor Cycle* for so many years, in his book *Motor Cycle Cavalcade* states that "he could personally identify two factors which saved the sport from collapse or anaemia. The first was the invention of the Simms-Bosch magneto ... the second was the energetic intervention of M J Schulte of the Triumph Cycle Company ... a man of great vigour, of cool and balanced judgement and of considerable prudence. He was the first cycle trade magnate to realise that a good motor cycle was likely to develop into the big brother of the pedal cycle, if it did not actually supersede the lighter machine...."

So, in the early years of the 20th century, Triumph was well established, with some good products and sound management. Edward Turner, who much later was to give us the Speed Twin, was then a little lad just about starting school...!

The First Thirty Years

In this relatively short period the motor cycle grew up from a bicycle with an engine attached, to what we could almost call the definitive motor cycle. At first designers were undecided as to the best position for the engine. Some mounted it over the front wheel where, presumably, it was thought that the rider could keep a watchful eye on it. From here it drove either the front wheel by a short belt, or the rear wheel by an enormously long belt. Other designers put the engine in front of the bottom bracket, between the bottom bracket and the rear wheel, under the saddle, on top of the front down tube and even behind the rear wheel. Finally, led probably by the Werner, the engine ousted the pedalling gear from the bottom bracket position and there it has stayed ever since. The obvious position, one would think, from a centre of gravity and weight distribution point of view, but it did not seem so obvious in those far-off days. The 1902 Triumph had its Minerva engine in front of the bottom bracket but it was not long before the pedalling gear was pushed back and the engine securely bolted in its final position at the bottom of the front down tube.

Triumph had its own engine by 1905, a 78 x 76mm (363cc) single cylinder side valve said to be the first successful engine with ball bearings to support the mainshaft. An output of 3hp at 1500 rpm was claimed. Two years later the engine increased in size to 453cc then to 476cc, in 1910 it was 499cc and finally in 1914 it reached 550cc, where it stayed until well into the 1920s.

By 1907 the company had outgrown the Much Park Street factory and a new location in Priory Street was added to the company's resources. This was right in the city centre near the cathedral and developed eventually into one of the biggest factories in the city.

Motor cycle competitions of various kinds had been organised right from the earliest days, long distance events to demonstrate reliability being particularly popular. Racing had started, Brooklands Track opened in 1907 and the first Isle of Man race was also held. Triumph finished second and third in the Isle of Man single cylinder class that year but won it very decisively the following year as well as clocking the fastest lap. In the meantime the Priory Street works was really getting into top gear to meet the demand for its products and production reached 3000 machines in 1909.

Bettmann had always taken a great interest in the civic affairs of his adopted city. He was a founder of the Chamber of Commerce, was elected to the City Council in 1907 and became Mayor in 1913/14. For a German to be Mayor of Coventry at the outbreak of war was a unique situation. His loyalty was to Britain and he not only ensured that the army got its motor cycles but also launched a range of charitable funds which raised large sums of money. He started a home for Belgian refugees, presided over recruiting meetings at the Drill Hall and took a major part in many other activities to promote the war effort. When war broke out the powers-that-be had not given much thought to motor cycles, which meant that anything on the factory floor that could be ridden was requisitioned. Oddly enough, exactly the same thing happened in the early days of the last war – we never learn! In the case of Triumph, large numbers of the 550cc free engine clutch with three-speed hub Type "A" were pressed into service. However something better was coming along and this was the famous Type "H" with a separate Sturmey Archer three-speed countershaft gearbox, clutch, chain primary drive and final belt. The modern motor cycle had almost arrived. Most manufacturers began to develop something similar and this format has remained to the present day – even belt drive is coming back. During the four years of war, Triumph supplied over 30,000 motor cycles to the British and Allied forces and it was on the battle fronts of Europe that the Type "H" earned the nickname "Trusty Triumph" – such was its reputation for reliable performance under appalling conditions.

The war introduced large numbers of young men to the experience of motoring on two wheels and four, and this was to operate much to the advantage of the twin industries when the soldiers returned home. They demanded transport for themselves and their families and factories were kept busy meeting this demand.

1903 TRIUMPH – JAP. This is probably the oldest Triumph in existence and is fitted with a 70 x 76mm (293cc) JAP single cylinder engine. It has an automatic inlet valve and a single tank-mounted lever which "controls simultaneously the throttle and ignition advance." Preserved in the National Motor Museum at Beaulieu.

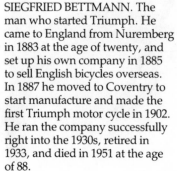

SIEGFRIED BETTMANN. The man who started Triumph. He came to England from Nuremberg in 1883 at the age of twenty, and set up his own company in 1885 to sell English bicycles overseas. In 1887 he moved to Coventry to start manufacture and made the first Triumph motor cycle in 1902. He ran the company successfully right into the 1930s, retired in 1933, and died in 1951 at the age of 88.

TRIUMPH NO. 1. This picture of the very first Triumph motor cycle (1902) has appeared many times before and in many publications. As it is a company-produced illustration, one must assume it to be authentic. It is actually a drawing, not a photograph, although it was probably based on a photograph originally. The general layout does bear a close resemblance to the 1903 Triumph in the museum at Beaulieu, although the engine is a Minerva whereas the Beaulieu machine has a JAP. Various makes of engine were tried in these early days until Triumph started to make their own in 1905.

1906 3hp. A redesigned frame bringing the top tube down to 31 inches from the ground was a significant step in shaking off the influence of the bicycle. The famous Triumph patented spring fork was fitted, which pivoted on a ball bearing at the crown with two springs at the top to control fore and aft movement. This unique design lasted well into the 1920s and worked quite effectively at the speeds of the day. The engine produced 3hp at 1500rpm and direct belt drive between the engine and the rear wheel provided a ratio of 4½:1. Throttle, ignition and air lever controls were mounted on the tank side with a cut-out on the left handlebar. This cut the ignition, with further movement lifting the exhaust valve. Price £43.

1905 TRIUMPH ENGINE. In 1905, Triumph started to make their own engine, which was a single cylinder side valve of 78 x 76mm (363cc), and the claim was made that this was the first engine "to which ball bearings have been successfully applied to the mainshaft, and not in a single instance have these bearings shown any wear, even after 10,000 miles." The valve gear was simple and substantial. The cams were cut out of the solid web of the gear wheels and bell crank levers were interposed between the cams and the tappets. Forged steel flywheels were fitted, with heavy rims.

MR F HULBERT. A formidable performer in competitions on his 3hp Triumph, in 1905 he took part in the ACC Hill Climb, the ACC Penalty Run, the MCC 200 Mile Non-Stop Run, the MCC London-Edinburgh, the Bexhill Race Meeting, the Muratti Trophy Trial, the ACC Six Days Trial and the Honiton and Reigate Hill Climbs, in all of which he finished at or close to the top. He was obviously a talented all-rounder and the performance of the Triumph complimented his efforts.

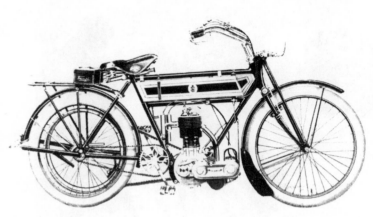

1907 3½hp. In this model the engine had increased in size to 82 x 86mm (453cc), producing an extra half horsepower at 1500rpm. The single gear ratio remained at 4½:1. The top tube of the frame was down another inch, which enabled the average rider to put his feet more firmly on the ground. As pedals became less of a necessity, the fact that the saddle was low did not matter too much. The chain driven magneto was a major reliability factor. This was a good, practical motor cycle and at £47.10.0d gave really good value.

1908 3½hp. The engine grew again to 84 x 86mm (476cc) and there were other valuable changes in this season. A Triumph-made carburettor was fitted and for the first time the controls were all moved to the handlebars (where they have remained ever since). A variable pulley was fitted giving ratios between 4 and 6:1. To vary the ratio, the rider had to stop, screw the flange of the pulley in or out as required, then adjust the length of the driving belt. Tedious, but preferable to pushing up the hill. An interesting refinement was the fitting of plain bearings to the pedal cranks – to prevent the cranks revolving when the machine was in motion. Price £48.

W CREYTON. The first single cylinder rider to complete the course in the 1910 Tourist Trophy Race. He finished third at 46.28mph on his 3½hp Tourist Trophy Racer. All eight starters riding this model finished the race.

JACK MARSHALL. Seen here after finishing second in the single cylinder class of the TT in 1907. The robust looking gentleman on the right is Mr Robert Todd, an official. Marshall won the race the following year, retired in 1909 and finished sixth in 1910. That was his last appearance in the Isle of Man. Later he became a publican in Coventry with a pub, The Royal Oak, not all that far away from the Triumph works – it is still there but the works are not.

1911 3½hp 499cc. This model was fitted with a "Patent Free Engine Plate Clutch" which permitted the rider to start from rest whilst seated in the saddle. Also, he could start up without running alongside and leaping into the saddle with the machine in motion. The clutch was incorporated in the rear wheel hub and was operated by a heel and toe pedal on the offside of the engine. This was a step forward in the evolution of the modern motor cycle, but it had not quite reached the hand-operated clutch and multi-speed gearbox stage, though these were not far off.

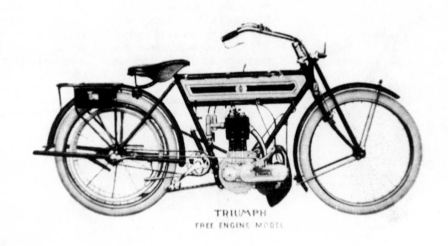

TRIUMPH
FREE ENGINE MODEL

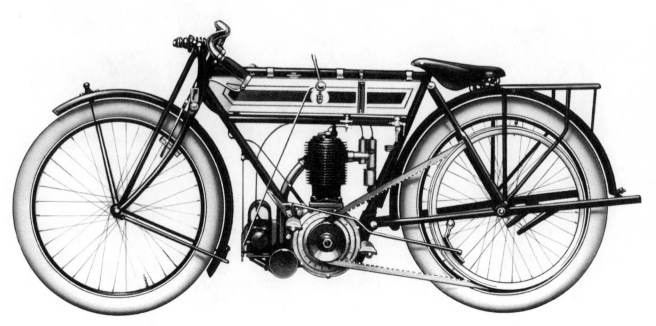

3½hp TOURIST TROPHY RACER. This is the model already referred to which in the 1910 TT had eight starters and eight finishers – 3rd, 4th, 6th, 7th, 8th, 11th, 13th and 15th, a quite remarkable record. A variable pulley was fitted giving ratios from 3¼ to 4½:1. No pedals were fitted. An extra low frame and specially shaped bars enabled the rider to "get down to it" and two sets of footrests gave a choice of position. A Bosch or Simms HT magneto looked after the ignition and the fuel tank held 1¼ gallons and a quart of oil.

11

TRIUMPH
T.T. ROADSTER

1912 3½hp TOURIST TROPHY ROADSTER. This model was very similar to the TT Racer but was equipped as a roadster. It had the shorter wheelbase of the racer but the handlebars and saddle were shaped for comfort rather than speed. No pedalling gear was fitted and two sets of footrests gave a choice of riding positions. A variable pulley provided ratios from 3¾ to 5:1 to be selected. The manufacturer's comment was, "This is a very fast machine combining the speed of the racing machine and the comfort, in respect to the equipment, of the touring mount." What more could you want?

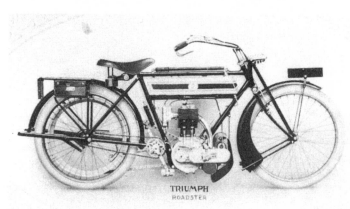

TRIUMPH
ROADSTER

TRIUMPH
FREE ENGINE MODEL

1912 3½hp ROADSTER. This model was at the bottom of the range for 1912 but it did have a variable pulley (4¼ to 6¼:1) and pedalling gear. The engine was the standard side valve of 85 x 88mm (499cc). The mudguarding, particularly at the front, was comprehensive and the magneto had its own protective mud flap. The makers claimed that it would crawl at five miles per hour and quickly accelerate to fifty. A good touring bike for the not-so-expert rider, being simple to operate and maintain, it had a good turn of speed when required. Price £48.15.0d.

1913 3½hp ROADSTER FREE ENGINE MODEL TYPE A. A popular model for touring, the free engine clutch (foot operated) making it easy to control in traffic or when starting off. The makers also suggest that "long hills can be coasted with the clutch disengaged, thus cooling the engine", a very dubious practice. There were two other variants to this model, the Type B, which did not have the free engine clutch, and the Type C which had a 3-speed hub gear. Prices: Type A £55.10.0d, Type B £49.5.0d, Type C £59.15.0d.

1914 4hp TYPE A ROADSTER FREE ENGINE MODEL. A useful tourer this, supplied in large numbers to the Forces in the initial stages of the Great War. The engine was the enlarged 85 x 97mm (550cc) single cylinder side valve with variable pulley (4¼ to 6¼:1), Triumph carburettor and Bosch high tension magneto. The free engine plate clutch was incorporated in the rear hub, operated by heel and toe pedal on the offside. Drive was by 7/8in rubber V belt and the Triumph patent spring fork was employed. Alternative specifications could be supplied a) omitting free engine clutch or b) with three-speed hub gear. A £10 variation in price covered the three specifications.

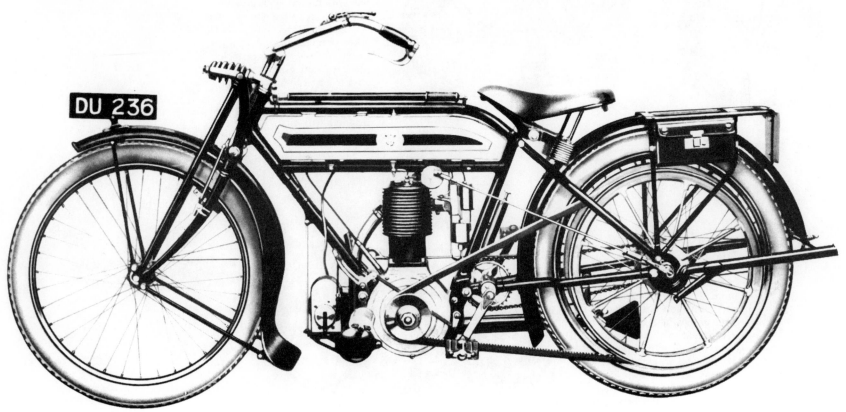

1915 3½hp TYPE H THREE-SPEED COUNTERSHAFT MODEL. This is an updated Type A still with final belt drive but now boasting a separate 3-speed Sturmey Archer countershaft gearbox in place of the archaic free engine clutch and variable pulley. At last the owner, with a proper clutch, can start and stop smoothly and climb all reasonable hills with the aid of his gearbox. The side valve engine went up in size to 85 x 97 (550cc), with shock absorber on the mainshaft and totally enclosed and adjustable primary chain. Gearbox ratios were 5, 8 and 13⅓:1, and a Triumph semi-automatic carburettor and chain-driven HT magneto were fitted.

TRIUMPH AT WAR. During the 1914-18 war, Triumph supplied motor cycles to the forces right from the start. By the finish the British Army had taken 30,000 and many more were used by allied armies. The model supplied in the greatest numbers was the 550cc Type H with 3-speed Sturmey Archer countershaft gearbox, but there were also many of the Type A with free engine clutch, a few being seen in this photograph.

The 1920s

This was the period during which Triumph finally shook off its belts and moved into the chain driven, overhead valve and internal expanding brake era. Even the traditional flat tank gave way to a saddle tank towards the end.

Schulte had left the company in 1919 after a disagreement with Bettmann. Schulte wanted to discontinue bicycle manufacture and move into cars. Colonel Holbrook took his place as General Manager. Bettmann had a high opinion of Holbrook when the latter was at the War Office and responsible for procuring motor cycles for the forces during the war. Holbrook agreed with Schulte about cars and the first Triumph car, with a Ricardo-designed engine, appeared in 1923.

There had been a downturn in trade following the unsettled conditions and raging inflation after the war, and it was to counter this that the famous (or notorious) model P was launched at the 1924 Show – a 500cc side valve at the incredible price of £42.17.6d., way below anything comparable on the market. The public responded enthusiastically and the demand put a strain on the workforce at Priory Street, but they were equal to the challenge and on occasions surprised themselves by turning out 1000 machines a week.

Regrettably the P did not reach the high standard which the public had come to expect from Triumph. With Schulte gone, all kinds of short cuts were made to get the price down – like discarding valve guides and running the valves direct in the cylinder material. The front brake was a joke, a piece of asbestos rope round a small diameter rim on the front wheel. How the directors, previously sticklers for quality, allowed such things to go through is incomprehensible. Schulte would never have agreed. Nothing could be done until the first 20,000 had been built and then the much improved Mark II appeared, which restored some of the faith lost by dealers and the public.

The overhead valve engine began to make its appearance in the 1920s and the first Triumph move in this direction was the Ricardo-developed four valve ohv type R – popularly known as the 'Riccy'. Triumph had entered a team in the 1921 Senior TT without giving any information on the machines they intended to use. The 550cc 4hp engine which was their main production type was too big to comply with ACU limits so that something new was known to be in the offing. When the TT model was described for the first time in *The Motor Cycle* of 2nd June 1921 it caused a sensation. The cylinder, valve gear and everything above the crankcase had been designed by Harry (later Sir Harry) Ricardo and embodied all the latest knowledge of the art: four overhead valves in a hemispherical head, a machined steel cylinder, aluminium piston and other advanced details. It did not do well first time out in the Island, only one finishing, in 16th place. However, the next year it came second in the Senior Race ridden by Walter Brandish, son of the Triumph dealer in Coventry. It appeared in the standard production range for 1922 but with a cast iron cylinder, and cost £120. Other successes and records were achieved but the company seemed to lose interest in the "Riccy" and very little further development followed. It was eventually superseded by the Victor Horsman two valve ohv, labelled the TT. This was a good looking, well engineered job on which Horsman broke many records. It was the Triumph No 1 until Val Page came along in 1932.

RIGHT IN THE CENTRE. The shaded area on this map of modern Coventry represents the approximate position of the Triumph factory before it was destroyed by enemy action in the great Coventry blitz of November 1940. From Cox Street at one end almost to Trinity Street at the other, it was an impressive place and a familiar one to residents of the city. Visitors to Coventry today standing by the great cathedral are on the spot where the famous H, the 'Riccy', the Speed Twin, the Tiger 100 and many others first powered their way on to the roads of Britain and the world.

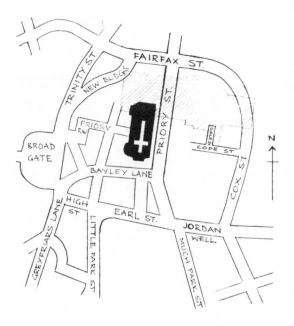

THE PRIORY STREET WORKS. This 1924 photograph shows a good part of the old Triumph factory but not quite all of it. The road in the centre dividing the two halves is Priory Street, with the swimming baths at the extreme left. The tall building in the distance is in Cox Street. Bettmann and Schulte moved to Coventry in 1889 and rented a small factory in Much Park Street. Business prospered, they started making motor cycles in 1902, they had their own engine by 1905 and the following year saw 500 machines completed. In 1907 they were bursting at the seams and moved to a new location in Priory Street, though still retaining the Much Park Street premises. Production increased and by 1925 the works occupied 500,000 square feet of floor space and employed 3000 people. The photographs which follow show the Priory Street works at this point. Some idea of its size can be judged by the length of the individual shops seen in the various photographs. Vast numbers of machine tools were employed, driven by belts from overhead shafting. It is interesting to recall that some of these tools survived the blitz, were rescued and installed in the new Meriden works, opened in 1942, where overhead shafting could be seen operating for some years after the war.

16

Main Machine Shop, Drilling
Section.

Main Machine Shop, Capstan
Section.

Main Machine Shop, Milling
Section.

Corner of the Grinding Shop.

Machine Shop, Cylinder and
Flywheel Group.

Finishing Shop, Engine
Assembly.

18

Final Assembly No 1 Shop.

Finishing Shop, Wiring Track.

Tool Room.

Frame Building Shop, frame
setting.

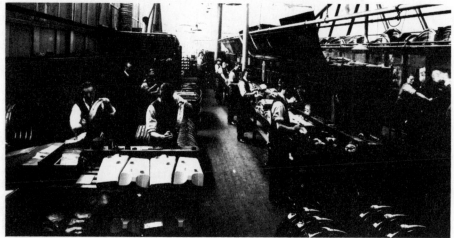

Enamelling Shop, lining.

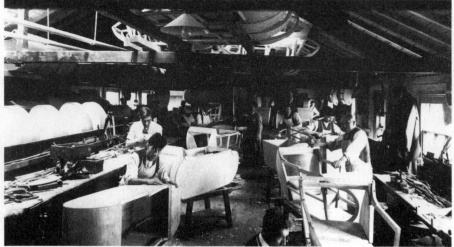

Sidecar Body Building Shop.

1922 4hp TYPE SD. This was a modernised version of the famous model H. Introduced in 1920, the SD had a 3-speed gearbox of Triumph design and manufacture, with a multi-plate clutch, oil bath primary chaincase and, at last, final chain drive. SD stood for Spring Drive, which was a shock absorber mounted on an extension of the gearbox mainshaft. The engine was the familiar 85 x 97mm, 550cc side valve with roller bearing big-end and decompressor. Other features included the Triumph semi-automatic carburettor, HT magneto and a hand lubricating pump. A popular sidecar mount, the SD stepped up its reliability rating in this field with the use of chain drive. Price £115.

1922 3½hp TYPE R FAST ROADSTER. As described in the introduction to this chapter, the Type R or "Riccy" had a four valve ohv head and steel barrel designed by Ricardo for the 1921 Senior TT. Only one finished in the race but in November of that year Major F B Halford broke the 500cc world hour record at 76.74mph on the "Riccy", along with the 50 miles standing start at 77.27mph and the one mile (flying) British record at 87.8mph. For production the barrel material was changed to cast iron with deeper finning. The rest of the machine was similar to the SD except that the Triumph hinged fork was changed to one of Druid design with side springs. The old to-and-fro Triumph fork could not cope with the speed of the "Riccy".

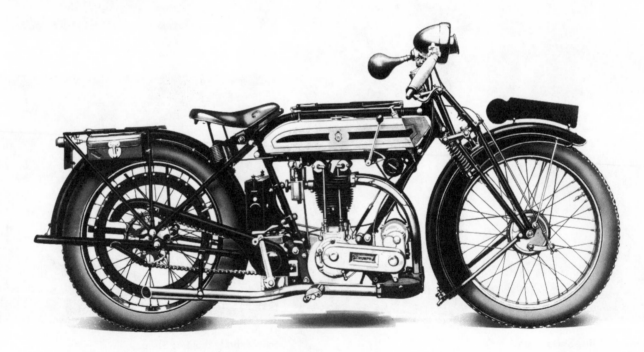

1922 2¼hp TYPE LW JUNIOR
MODEL. Launched in November
1913, the Junior was a complete
departure from normal Triumph
practice. It was a two-stroke of
64 x 70mm (225cc) with a
countershaft 2-speed gear, but no
clutch. Primary drive was by
chain, final drive by V belt. The
gears were controlled by a cable
from a handlebar lever, the rider
engaging low gear and paddling
off, which started the engine. The
fuel tank was cylindrical and
carried both petrol and oil; the
latter could be drawn off into a
measure incorporated in the filler
cap to produce the petroil mixture
(4 measures to a gallon).
Although named "Junior" by the
company, the public insisted on
calling it the "Baby Triumph" and
that stuck. Price £65.

1922 4hp TRIUMPH AND
GLORIA SIDECAR No 9.
Triumph made their own sidecars
and they were offered as an outfit
with either the Type H (chain-
cum-belt) or the SD (all-chain).
The body was coachbuilt,
upholstered in antique Pegamoid
cloth, painted Parma violet with
black beading, panelled in
lavender grey and lined in
bronze. The chassis was rigidly
attached at four points but could
be detached quickly and simply.
Springs were inverted half elliptic
at rear, coil in front. Tyre size was
26 x 2½ as on the motor cycle.
Prices: with Type H £145, with
Type SD £155.

1922 4hp TRIUMPH WITH COMMERCIAL SIDECAR No 9a. Like the passenger sidecar the commercial box was offered either with the chain-cum-belt Type H or the all-chain SD. Details of the chassis and attachments were identical. The box body was coachbuilt, painted Parma violet, and lined in bronze and black. Outside measurements were 22in wide by 22½in deep by 51in long. This is an interesting combination which belongs strictly to the past – commercial sidecars are virtually unknown today. Prices: with Type H £140, with Type SD £150.

1924 550cc TYPE SD. In this later SD some notable differences can be seen compared with earlier models. An internal-expanding front brake (of modest proportions) replaces the bicycle-type rim brake. The old Triumph pivoted fork has gone and the substantial replacement, made under Druid patents, has side springs. Electric lighting and electric horn are also offered. In official company literature, the old 4hp classification was changed to 5.50hp based on the 550cc capacity of the engine, a simple way of picking up an extra 1½ horsepower.

499cc TYPE R. Similar changes can be seen in the famous "Riccy" – the internal expanding front brake, the electrics, etc. The Druid-type front fork was fitted right from the start as the old pivoted fork was abandoned at the debut of the "Riccy" in the 1921 Isle of Man races, when the riders had complained about the handling, not surprising in view of the extra performance of the "Riccy" compared with the old side-valvers.

1924 346cc TYPE LS. Introduced in 1923 as a last-minute show sensation the LS was something quite out of Triumph mainstream design. It was a 350cc side valve single with a 3-speed gearbox built in unit with the engine, and had a gear primary drive, all metal (steel and copper) clutch, mechanical force feed lubrication and internal-expanding brakes on both wheels. The rear wheel brake reverted to a dummy belt rim when the LS finally went into production some twelve months later. It was years ahead of its time, but did not sell, possibly for that reason, and faded out after 1927.

1924 550cc DE LUXE
COMBINATION. The sidecar
combination was the family car of
the 1920s, and although the
powerful big twin of 800/1000cc
was the obvious choice if one
could afford it, many could not,
and the 4hp or 500/600cc model
was the alternative. Triumph
were in this category and the
550cc side valve SD with final
chain drive was a popular
machine. The pulling power of
this engine was legendary and it
would climb anything, perhaps
not very quickly, but very surely.
A few changes can be noted over
the earlier models. C springs
replace coils at the front and the
lamp on the mudguard has
grown in size. The motor cycle
has Druid-type forks and an
internal-expanding front brake.

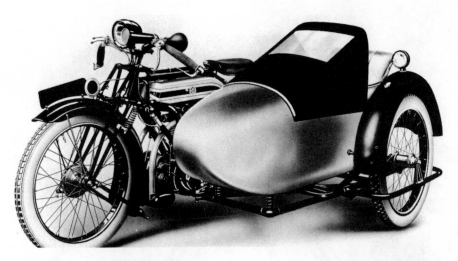

1924 499cc SUPER COMBINATION. For the sporting sidecarist this outfit must have had many attractions. Nicely shaped, light in weight and coupled to the celebrated four valve "Riccy", its performance must have been impressive in its day. Triumph made all their own sidecars and the workmanship and finish were of a very high order. Even so, you could have bought this top-of-the-range sidecar and still had some change out of £20. The "Riccy" attached to it would add around £120 to the price. Strangely, the 1922 catalogue announcing the Type R for the first time says "the Type R is strictly a solo mount and we do not recommend the fitting of a sidecar to this model." Yet two years later you could buy the "Riccy" complete with chair.

TRIUMPH DIRECTORS, 1925. Bettmann, Fridlander and Schloss were all Germans. Schloss came from Nuremberg, like Bettmann, and there is a story that when he was promoted to manage the London office he asked if he could invest his savings, some £100, in the company. Bettmann was so pleased by this that he offered him a directorship. Schulte agreed but warned Bettmann not to scatter directorships around quite so freely. Lord Leigh was an important Warwickshire landowner whose stately home, Stoneleigh Abbey, has recently been opened to the public. Lt. Colonel Holbrook had dealings with Bettmann over the supply of motor cycles to the forces during the Great War and was invited to join the company afterwards. As Colonel Sir Claude Vernon

Holbrook, he was at various times Deputy Lieutenant of Warwickshire, a magistrate and a county councillor. He died in 1979 at the age of 93.

1925 494cc MODEL P. This was the model that really set the industry alight in 1925 when it was offered for £42.17.6d, making it was far and away the cheapest 500 on offer at that time. The price cutting was deliberate policy, and there were several suspect items in the specification which had to be modified urgently, though not until the initial batch of 20,000 had been built. The front brake, the clutch operation and the big-end all gave trouble and the absence of valve guides – the valve stems ran direct in the cylinder casting – was a dubious economy. Most of these problems were rectified in the Mark II towards the end of 1925 and the P finally took its place as a respectable member of the Triumph family.

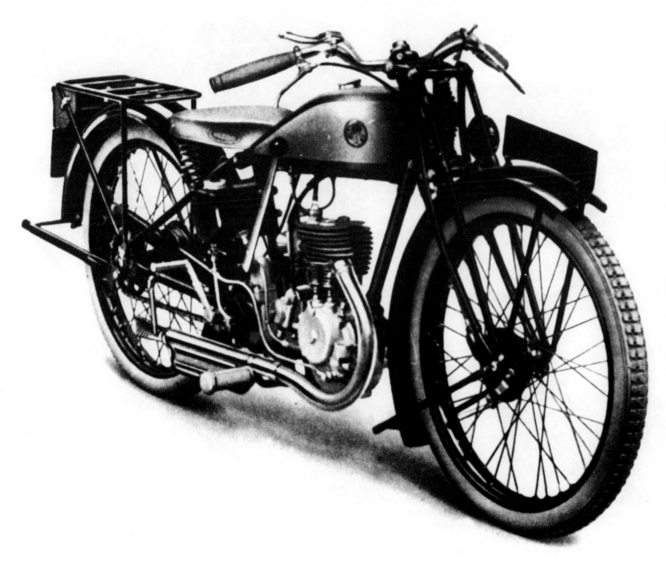

1929 277cc MODEL WS. This model, introduced initially as the W in 1927, sought to pack the most possible punch into a motor cycle weighing less than the 200lb taxation mark, hence the peculiar capacity. The WS was given a saddle tank and with this and the optional Lucas Magdyno electrical equipment it exceeded the 200lb limit, although it was inside it if fitted with an acetylene set. It had a single cylinder side valve engine of 66.5 x 80mm (277.8cc), adjustable tappets, decompressor, adjustable oil pump and sight feed with independent feed for auxiliary foot pump. The specification included a 3-speed hand-controlled gearbox, 1½ gallon fuel tank, Triumph girder forks, Dunlop 26 x 2.75 wired tyres, and internal expanding brakes front and rear. Chromium plating was extra.

1929 350cc ohv CO. After cutbacks in the previous years to enable the works to concentrate on getting a car on the market, 1929 saw eight models in the range again with the C Group comprising the 550cc side valve CSD, the 498cc side valve CN and the 350cc ohv CO. The latter was a robust looking two port single 72 x 85mm (348cc) with pushrod-operated overhead valves, the valve gear being totally enclosed. It had a roller bearing big-end with pressure oil feed, semi-dry sump lubrication, Amal carburettor and magneto ignition. The gearbox had three speeds, 5.18, 7.71 and 12.23:1, and was hand-controlled. Also featured were a cradle-type frame with girder forks, 2½ gallon tank, 26 x 3.25 wired-type Dunlop tyres, and internal expanding brakes front and rear.

1929 494cc NL. One is inclined to suspect that this was a slightly modernised P. It had the same 84 x 89mm side valve engine. The front brake was the "internal-expanding ring-type with slight servo action" as fitted to the MK II P. The appearance was much improved, though, with a saddle tank, and the forks had a central tension spring in place of the two side springs. Dunlop wired-type tyres replaced the beaded edge, and it was the only model in the range to retain the Triumph carburettor. There was a three-speed gearbox with tankside quadrant (ratios 5.06, 8.2, 14.2:1), all-chain drive with helical cam type shock absorber on the engine shaft, high tension magneto and 2½ gallon fuel tank.

1929 498cc CN. This was an even more modernised side valve than the NL. The saddle tank and cradle frame looked good and the brakes were of some size, with special "tangential brake anchorages". The engine was of 80 x 99mm (497.5cc) with aluminium piston, roller bearing big-end with pressure oil feed, semi-dry sump lubrication, Amal carburettor, and high tension magneto. This model had all-chain drive with shock absorber in the rear wheel, six spring clutch with dry multi-friction discs, a 3-speed gearbox with tankside quadrant (ratios 5.04, 8.16, 14.03:1) and main and layshafts on roller bearings, 2½ gallon fuel tank, single tension spring girder forks with steering damper, Dunlop 26 x 3.25in wired tyres, and internal-expanding brakes front and rear.

1929 549cc NSD. The 550cc side valve Triumph had been a classic in the range since the days of the H. This one had a different bore/stroke ratio (84 x 99mm, 548.5cc) from the H, which was of 85 x 97mm. The front silencer rather spoilt the appearance and the internal spring ring-type front brake, of doubtful efficiency, came from the P. The specification included Amal carburettor, high tension magneto, shock absorber on the engine shaft, three-speed gearbox with tankside quadrant (ratios 5.06, 8.2, 14.12:1), all-chain drive, diamond-type frame, girder forks with central tension spring and steering damper, 2½ gallon fuel tank and Dunlop 26 x 3.25 wired-type tyres.

1929 549cc CSD. The CSD was basically similar to the 500cc CN but had the 84 x 99mm (548.5cc) side valve engine. Primarily intended for the family sidecar man, the CSD was a worthy successor to the earlier Triumph 550cc side valves. It was notably successful in powering the AA mobile patrol box sidecars.

1929 498cc ohv ST. Victor Horsman, the great tuner, rider, record breaker and, later, dealer in Liverpool, developed a 500cc ohv engine. This became the Type TT in 1927 and ran parallel with the "Riccy" until the latter faded out at the end of the season. The TT was a two port ohv of 80 x 99mm (499cc) with dry sump lubrication, Amal carburettor, HT magneto, 3-speed hand-operated gearbox (ratios 4.39, 6.52, 10.19:1), diamond frame, girder forks, Dunlop 26 x 3.25 tyres and 2½ gallon fuel tank. The TT later became the ST which was a good, solid 500 with a useful performance and up-to-date specification.

1929 TRIUMPH MOTOR CYCLES

EXPORT OR DIE! This phrase, bandied about after World War Two, tended to suggest that exporting was something new, which was nonsense. Triumph were great exporters and it may surprise some to learn that the 1929 catalogue had editions in Bulgarian, Danish, Dutch, German, Japanese, Portuguese, Italian, French, Spanish, plus English versions for Australia and India. Now that the British industry is largely Japanese, these pages from the 1929 Japanese edition should be readily understood in the U.K!

輸　入　元

製造元

大英國コヴェントリー市

トライアンフ自轉車製造會社

會株
社式
丸石商會京城支店
朝鮮京城府黄金町一丁目
電話本局（国）二六五〇六番

會株
社式
丸石商會福岡支店
九州福岡市下奥堂町十一
電話（国）七十六番

會株
社式
丸石商會名古屋支店
名古屋市西尾上町四丁目
電話東（国）三五九七番

會株
社式
丸石商會横濱支店
横濱市中區本町五丁目
電話長者町（25）（国）〇〇九〇番

會株
社式
丸石商會東京支店
東京市神田區今川橋
電話神田（25）（3）二〇〇番

會株
社式
丸石商會大阪本店
大阪市西區新町北通
電話新町（国）一〇六六五四三番

TRIUMPH

Take-over in the 1930s

The depression of the early 1930s had a disastrous effect on Triumph and drastic steps were necessary to remain in business. Lloyds Bank appointed a Mr Graham as Manager, Bettmann was demoted from Managing Director to Vice-Chairman, and in 1935 it was decided to sell off the Priory Street works, finish with motor cycles and concentrate on cars in a factory recently acquired in the Foleshill Road, Coventry. Jack Sangster, who had rescued the Ariel company from a similar situation in 1932, moved in swiftly and did a deal with Graham. He took over the manufacturing rights of the motor cycles, the Priory Street works and such machinery and equipment as were required. The name of a non-trading subsidiary was adopted – Triumph Engineering Co. Ltd – first registered on 23rd April 1906 with £100 capital, increased to £21,000 on 25th February 1936. The agreement was finally completed on 22nd January 1936. The cars and motor cycles now went their separate ways, the bicycles having been disposed of two years before. At this point Sangster asked Bettmann to become Chairman of Triumph Engineering, to which he readily assented. This was an astute move by Sangster as Bettmann was much respected by both suppliers and dealers, and confidence in the new organisation was greatly strengthened by the appointment. His tenure as Chairman lasted only until the company was well established, which did not take long.

The Sangster family had been in the business from the early days of the Ariel organisation and "Mr Jack", himself an engineer, had designed a light two cylinder motor car which the Rover Company took up and put into production as the Rover Eight. At Triumph Sangster inherited some well engineered motor cycles designed by Val Page, who had moved to Triumph from Ariel in 1932. There was a complete range of single cylinder models, both overhead and side valve, plus the 6/1, an impressive 650cc vertical twin. These were introduced at the 1933 Olympia Show for the 1934 season and remained largely unchanged through 1935 to the time of the take-over.

In the meantime Ariel's Development Engineer, one Edward Turner, who had joined Ariel in 1928, moved into Page's seat there as Chief Designer. He was at the time developing his Square Four Ariel. Sangster was still boss of Ariel and he now moved Turner to Triumph as Chief Designer and Managing Director. Page left, going over to BSA where he worked on the M20 and Gold Star. He later returned to Ariel, and the revolutionary Ariel Leader range was a fitting final tribute to the career of one of the industry's most talented designers.

Turner went to work at once to reduce the multiplicity of component parts, simplify and rationalise manufacture and eliminate unprofitable projects. At the same time something had to be done quickly to present some sparkling new models to the public. So he took three of Page's singles, the 5/5 (500cc), the 3/2 (350cc) and the L2/1 (250cc) and with little mechanical change but with what we would today call cosmetic treatment he turned them into the Tiger 90, the Tiger 80 and the Tiger 70. Sporty names and a lot of showroom glitter did the trick and the dealers were in business again. The L2/1 was soon replaced by the 2/1 as the latter had many parts in common with the 3/2 and was a more economic proposition. The L2/1 was a superb little motor cycle but Turner claimed he was giving away a fiver in the toolbox of every one!

But Turner had by no means finished yet, and his next offering changed the course of motor cycle design world-wide for the next thirty years. This was the 500cc Speed Twin, displayed at the 1937 Show for the 1938 season. It was Turner's masterpiece. Triumph already had a vertical twin in the range, Page's 6/1, but it was essentially a sidecar mount, a job which it did very well. It was not what Turner wanted and it faded from the range. The Speed Twin bore no resemblance to the 6/1 apart from the fact that the pistons went up and down together. The engine is so familiar today that it is not necessary to go into any great detail here except to state that it had a central flywheel and camshafts mounted fore and aft of the crankcase, operating the valves through short pushrods. The remainder of the machine was basically Tiger 90, and it is interesting to note that with the twin cylinder engine the weight of the whole machine showed no increase over the Tiger 90. Its performance was startling though, a fact which road tests by the motor cycling journals soon confirmed. Triumph was on its way back in no uncertain manner.

1935 500cc 5/2. Val Page had joined Triumph as Chief Designer in 1932 and had produced a first class range of modern motor cycles. In the 1935 range there were three ohv 500s. In order of performance potential the 5/2 was bottom of the list, although in practice there was probably not a lot to choose between it and the 5/5. The 5/10 was a racer and in a different category altogether. The 5/2 had a compression ratio of 6.5:1, the 5/5 7:1. The 5/2 had 7 inch brakes, the 5/5 8 inch, and so on. The engine was a single cylinder two port ohv of 84 x 89mm (493cc) with dry sump lubrication. Carburation was by Amal, with a 6v Lucas Magdyno to take care of the electrics, and there was a 4-speed gearbox with tankside change (foot control £1 extra) and ratios of 4.70, 5.65, 8.5 and 13.2:1. At last a Triumph with four speeds! Page's designs brought Triumph right up to date and were the basis of Triumph practice for many years ahead.

1935 250cc L2/1. The L2/1 was an exceptionally good motor cycle but it was expensive to make and unprofitable. At £40.10s. this is not surprising. It had a unique integrally-forged flywheel and mainshaft set-up, which was the best of its kind, a fact recognised by competition riders who extracted remarkable performances from the engine, which was a 249cc single cylinder pushrod ohv of 63 x 80mm (the same bore and stroke as the later Speed Twin). The specification included dry sump lubrication, Lucas Magdyno, 4-speed gearbox with tankside change (foot control £1 extra) and ratios of 6.10, 7.32, 10.55 and 15.5:1, cradle frame, girder forks and 6 inch internal-expanding brakes.

1935 250cc 2/1. When Val Page set about re-vamping the Triumph range in 1932, he insisted on a high degree of commonality in the specifications. Thus, the 250s, 350s and 500s were virtually the same motor cycle except for their engines. This was good for production but the smaller models tended to look overweight, which was not a serious fault as the quality was there and they were well engineered. The 2/1 had a 63 x 80mm (249cc) single cylinder engine with totally enclosed, lubricated valve gear. It was a completely different engine to the L2/1 (the odd man out) but was virtually identical to its larger partners. Later it became Turner's Tiger 70.

1935 550cc 5/1. 550cc side valves had a long history at Triumph going back to the 1914-18 war. This 1935 model was eyeable, robust and well made. The hand-change was outdated but one could pay an extra £1 for foot control. The engine was a conventional single cylinder 84 x 99mm (549cc) with enclosed valves, an aluminium cylinder head, dry sump lubrication, Amal carburettor, Lucas Magdyno lighting, 4-speed gearbox, duplex cradle frame, girder fork, 7 inch brakes, and Dunlop 26 x 3.5 tyres. The price was £55.

1935 350cc 3/1. This was one of Val Page's models that possibly suffered through having its 350cc side valve engine slotted into the frame and running gear of a 500. Its performance could not have been spectacular. Nevertheless it was a sound and serviceable motor cycle and as the catalogue says "A model ideally suited for all round touring conditions". The 70 x 89mm (349cc) engine had an aluminium cylinder head, enclosed valves, dry sump lubrication, Amal carburettor and Lucas Magdyno.

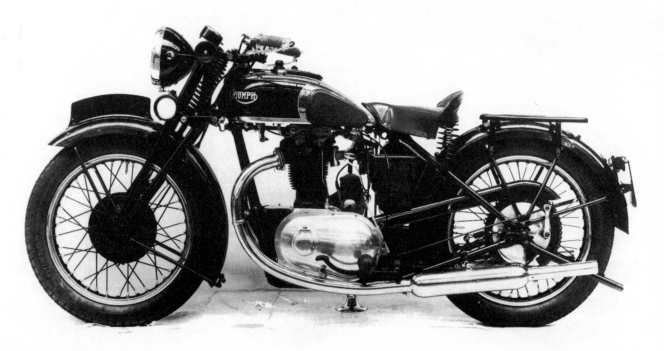

1935 650cc 6/1. This was Val Page's flagship. Many people are surprised to learn that Triumph had a vertical twin before Turner's Speed Twin came along. The 6/1 was a 360 degree twin and that was about the only point of similarity with Turner's twins. This engine had a single camshaft at the rear of the block and the valves were operated by unequal length pushrods working in a tunnel cast in the block. This was the arrangement adopted by BSA and Norton many years later. A 4-speed gearbox was bolted to the engine and was driven by helical gears without an intermediate gear so that the engine ran "backwards". The 6/1 was reputed to be "unburstable", a point made in 1933 when a 6/1 outfit ridden by Harry Perrey won a silver medal in the ISDT and then covered 500 miles in 500 minutes at Brooklands to win the Maudes Trophy.

1935/36 CONTROL LAYOUT. Triumph were strictly conventional in their mid-thirties arrangement of controls. The right handlebar carried a twist grip throttle with the cable running parallel with the bar, an inverted front brake lever, horn push and air lever. The left side had an inverted valve lifter control, clutch lever, ignition lever and dip switch. The speedometer was mounted behind the headlamp where it was readily visible and the steering damper knob was just behind it. Everything else – the ammeter, lighting switch, inspection lamp and oil pressure indicator – was on the tank top.

1935 6/1 650cc ENGINE. In this offside view of the 6/1 vertical twin engine can be seen the gear drive to the camshaft and Magdyno, also the flat area at the rear to which the 4-speed gearbox was bolted. In the other view the general layout of the engine is clear. Note the oil filler cap at the front.

1935 500cc 5/5. The 5/5 was the top performing 500 in the range apart from the 5/10, which was essentially a racer. The specification was almost identical to the 5/2, except that the compression ratio was 7:1, upswept exhaust pipes were optional, footchange was standard, the interconnected brakes were 8 inch diameter and the headlamp all chrome. Price £66.

1933 XV/1, X05/1, X05/5. A
Triumph with a Villiers engine?
This was true. It happened
because in the 1932 Budget
taxation by weight was scrapped
and engine capacity substituted.
The cheapest rate was 15/– for
150cc and below. It came into
force on 1st January 1933 and
there was a rush by
manufacturers to take advantage
of this new concession. Triumph
came up with two models, 98cc

and 150cc, at £16.16s and £21. The obvious place to go for engines was Villiers, who had them ready and waiting. This was an interim measure and Triumph soon designed a sloping 147cc ohv engine to go in the frame of the two-stroke. Unusually, the fins on the cylinder barrel were set parallel to the ground. There were two versions, the X05/1 and the sporting X05/5.

1935 500cc 5/10. If production racing had been invented, the Triumph 5/10 would certainly have qualified for inclusion. Basically it had the standard 84 x 89mm (493cc) two port single cylinder engine with 7:1 compression ratio but with forged disc flywheels, steel alloy connecting rod machined all over, and lightened reciprocating parts including tappets, pushrods and overhead rockers. The cylinder head and ports were polished and there was a choice of gear ratios. Its maximum was close to the magic 100mph and it handled well. Brakes were 8 inches in diameter with forged steel drums. The fuel tank held 3 gallons but a 4 gallon tank was available for £4 extra. Also specified were a 7 pint oil tank, Dunlop ribbed 27 x 3 front tyre and 27 x 3.25 rear. In 1934 Triumph entered a team in the Senior TT using the 5/10 but all retired with various problems – maybe they raced the 5/10 too soon because the bugs were soon sorted out and it became reasonably competitive thereafter.

J Y SANGSTER. Jack Sangster, who so effectively rescued Triumph from extinction in 1936, had done much the same for Ariel some years earlier when they, too, were in difficulties. His family had been associated with the industry for a very long time and "Mr Jack" or "JYS" as he was known eventually sold both Ariel and Triumph to the BSA Group, Ariel in 1939 and Triumph in 1951. He joined the Board of BSA and then became its Chairman in 1956. In 1960 he retired and handed the Group over to his successor with record profits of £3,500,000. His association with Edward Turner as designer resulted in some very fine motor cycles for both Ariel and Triumph.

EDWARD TURNER. Turner joined Ariel in 1928 with an impressive 350 ohc single which he had designed and built himself. Nothing came of it and he went on to produce the famous Ariel Square Four. Moving to Triumph in 1936 he revamped their range very successfully and topped it by producing the Speed Twin, which altered the whole course of motor cycle design world-wide. He was Managing Director of Triumph through the fifties and sixties when the company reached its peak with the Thunderbird, Tiger 110 and Bonneville as stars of the Turner era.

C W F PARKER. Charles Parker, Director and Secretary of Triumph virtually from start to finish, came from the Midlands staff of *Motor Cycling* but was in reality a trained accountant, not a journalist. He kept an unerring eye on the pennies and Triumph returned handsome profits during the whole of his time.

1938 250cc TIGER 70. The smallest of the three Tigers, the 70 started life based on the L2/1, but the L2/1 had certain features which made it expensive to produce, so after twelve months the Tiger 70 treatment was transferred to the 2/1, which had many parts common with the larger models. It had a single cylinder, single port ohv engine of 63 x 80mm (249cc), compression ratio 7.7:1, developing 16bhp at 5800rpm, dry sump lubrication, and Magdyno lighting and ignition. The 4-speed footchange gearbox had ratios of 5.8, 6.95, 10.0 and 14.7:1. Weight fully equipped was 310lb. Price £55.

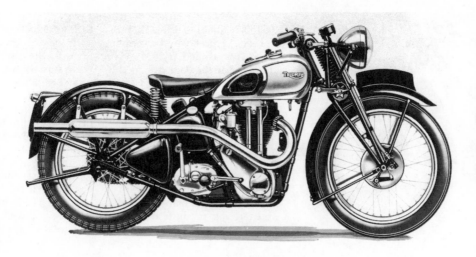

1938 350cc TIGER 80. The Tiger 80 was based on the previous 350cc 3/2 and the specification was much the same as the Tiger 70. The engine was of 70 x 89mm (349cc), compression ratio 7.5:1, developing 20bhp at 5700rpm. Gear ratios were 5.23, 6.28, 9.05 and 13.3:1. Weight fully equipped was 320lb. Price £61.

1938 500cc TIGER 90. The Tiger 90 was a development of the earlier 5/5 and the Tiger treatment made it a very attractive motor cycle. The engine of all the Tigers were individually tuned and Heenan and Froude brake tested, dismantled, inspected and re-assembled by expert mechanics. The 90 had a single cylinder, single port ohv engine of 84 x 89mm (497cc), compression ratio 7.08:1, developing 28.29bhp at 5800rpm. Cylinder head, connecting rod and flywheel peripheries were highly polished. It had dry sump lubrication, enclosed overhead valve gear, a large bore Amal carburettor, 6v Magdyno, and a 4-speed footchange gearbox with ratios of 4.78, 5.75, 8.26 and 12.1:1 a brazed full cradle frame, taper tube girder fork incorporating dampers with finger adjustment, 7 inch brakes front and rear and weighed 365lb. Price £70.

1938 500cc SPEED TWIN. There had been vertical twins before the Speed Twin arrived. In 1934 Triumph had the Page-designed 6/1, which was – to quote Edward Turner – "an extremely good machine from an engineering point of view". It did not set the world on fire. The Speed Twin was an entirely different proposition and it *did* set the world on fire. Such was its impact that virtually every other British manufacturer and many foreign were forced to produce something similar, although the war delayed their introduction. The Speed Twin was exhibited at the 1937 Show for the first time and at £75 was a sure winner. The engine was a beautifully symmetrical design with camshafts fore and aft of the block and centrally-disposed pushrods in plated tubes. The valve gear was totally enclosed and the camshafts were gear-driven, as was the Magdyno. Running on pre-war fuel, the engine produced 28.5bhp at 6000rpm. The frame, forks and running gear were identical with those of the Tiger 90.

1938 TIGER COMPETITION MODELS. The new company entered enthusiastically into the trials world and were consistently successful with riders like Allan Jefferies, Ted Thacker and Fred Povey. This experience was put to good use when competition versions of the Tigers were offered to the public. Specially tuned engines, choice of gear ratios, extra ground clearance, crankcase shields, upswept pipes, competition tyres, and a quickly-removable headlamp with plug and socket connection were among the special items included. The author bought a Comp Tiger 80 new in 1938 and used it in many S.E. Centre events where it did all that could be expected of it. If the owner had only been as good as the bike they might have won a few pots. Prices: Tiger 70 £62, Tiger 80 £68, Tiger 90 £77.

1938 500cc DE LUXE 5H. For his 500s (the Speed Twin, Tiger 90 and 5H) Turner specified identical forks, wheels, brakes, frames, tanks, etc., as part of the cost-cutting exercise. Twin port heads were abandoned as were twin front down tubes. All had the same gearbox – where no provision was made for hand-change! The 5H was a development of the previous 5/4 and the engine followed similar lines. It was a single cylinder ohv of 84 x 89mm (497cc), compression ratio 6:1, developing 23bhp at 5000rpm. It had dry sump lubrication, Amal carburettor, gear-driven 6v Lucas Magdyno lighting and ignition, a 4-speed gearbox with ratios of 4.78, 5.75, 8.26 and 12:1, brazed cradle frame, taper tube girder fork with finger adjustment to the dampers, and 7 inch brakes. Weight fully equipped was 365lb. Price £63.

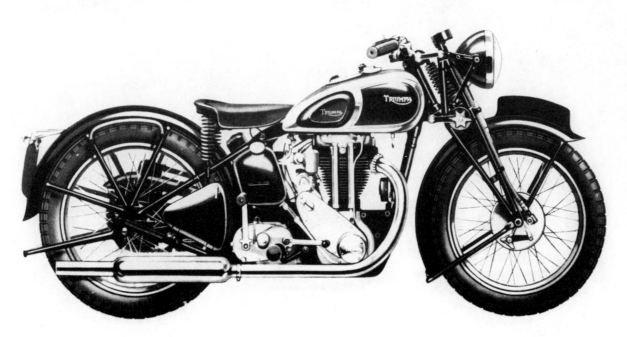

1938 350cc DE LUXE 3H. The 3H was distantly related to the earlier 3/2 and 3/5 models but now followed the trend set by the rest of the range – single port head, single tube frame, new gearbox and the shapely Turner tanks, toolbox and chaincase. It had a single cylinder engine of 70 x 89mm (349cc), compression ratio 6.7:1, developing 17bhp at 5200rpm, dry sump lubrication, gear-driven 6v Lucas Magdyno lighting and ignition, and a 4-speed footchange gearbox with ratios of 5.5, 6.6, 9.5 and 14.0:1. Weight was 320lb. Price £56.

1938 250cc DE LUXE 2H and 2HC. This was identical to the 3H apart from the 63 x 80mm (249cc) engine, compression ratio 6.92:1, developing 13bhp at 5200rpm.

Weight was 310lb. Price £51. The 2HC specified coil ignition and could be had for £48, making it the cheapest model in the range.

1938 350cc 3S (right) and 600cc 6S (above right). These two side valve machines were the last of a traditional Triumph type which dated back to the earliest days of the century. Turner brought them up to date in the same way as he had the ohv models. They had the Turner tanks, frames, forks, wheels and brakes but the engines were little altered except that the bigger one was increased in capacity from the old Triumph 550cc to 600cc. The 6S engine developed 18bhp at 4800rpm and the 3S produced 12bhp at the same rpm. Both models had 4-speed gearboxes, 26 x 3.25 tyres front and rear and 7 inch brakes. Weight: 6S 360lb, 3S 315lb. Prices: 6S £61, 3S £53. There was also a coil ignition alternative for the 3H labelled 3HC at £50.

1938 SIDECARS. Like the side valve engines by which they were usually towed, sidecars had been made by Triumph for a very long time, and like the side valve engines they did not survive the war. By that time the sidecar had lost much of its appeal as an economical passenger vehicle and the advent of the Mini and other small cars sealed its fate, at least as far as Triumph was concerned. It did survive elsewhere in a limited way. In 1938 Triumph offered four models, three open

and one described as a "sun saloon". Prices ranged from £20 to £23.15s. The chassis was a heavy gauge weldless tubular construction, with all lugs brazed. Fittings were Triumph made and the ball joints were self-aligning. Quarter elliptic springs supplied the suspension. The bodies were well made, comfortably upholstered in good quality materials and efficiently sprung. There were two colour schemes, Plum and Blue/Silver.

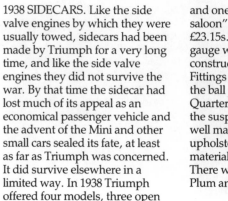

1939 500cc TIGER 100. In 1939 Turner started a model policy which he maintained right to the end. He introduced a new model in a fairly normal state of tune and augmented it later with a high performance sports model. The new Tiger 100 was a really quick version of the Speed Twin, just as years later the Tiger 110 supplemented the Thunderbird. Other models followed the same routine. The Tiger 100 had 8:1 forged slipper pistons and highly polished ports and internals. A bronze head could be had for an extra £5. The finish was similar to the Tiger singles chrome tanks with silver sheen panels lined in dark blue, and silver sheen mudguards with black centre lines. The wheels were similar and the 8 inch headlamp chrome plated. A nice touch was the detachable end portions of the silencers, which when removed left megaphones suitable for racing.

PRIORY STREET ASSEMBLY TRACK. Here we see some of the earliest Speed Twins being assembled at the Priory Street works before the war. In the 1920s, at least judging by the photographs, machines were assembled individually by one man on his own bench. The track scheme, with each man adding certain parts and moving the machine on to the next man as here, speeded up the process. The stores which fed out the parts to the track can just be seen on the extreme right.

The War Years

The years preceding the outbreak of war were again busy ones at Priory Street. Fortunately, among the works staff was one-time Machine Shop Superintendent Alfred Camwell, who eventually became Works Director and held that position until he retired in 1950. On him fell the task of organising Priory Street to produce the revamped and new models evolved by Edward Turner, and a very good job he made of it. "Alf" was a well liked and respected member of the Triumph family.

There was a healthy demand for the new models, and as it had done in P days Priory Street delivered the goods. Money began to flow into the company's coffers, a thing which had not happened on the same scale for some years. In charge of this side of the business was Charles Parker, Director and Secretary, a man who knew where every penny went and was happy to record a healthy profit every year for the next thirty years or so.

When war broke out in September 1939, Triumph (and others) were called upon to supply the forces with motor cycles and the 350cc and 500cc side valve models 3S and 5S were chosen to become the 3SW and the 5SW. These were similar in many ways to the side valve 16H Norton and M20 BSA already in military service.

Some time prior to the war the Government had asked manufacturers to produce prototypes of new army machines to conform to a specification that they supplied, one requirement of which was a 250lb weight limit. Turner designed a light 350cc twin with a three-speed gearbox in unit with the engine. It also had an alternator to provide lighting, the first time such an arrangement had been used. It is now universal on both cars and motor cycles and provides all electrical requirements. Other manufacturers produced their prototypes for test but Triumph was finally chosen and passed for production and a pilot batch got under way.

Then came 14th November 1940, when the German air force attacked Coventry with something like 400 planes and left the city centre, including the Triumph works, a heap of smouldering rubble. The pilot batch of the 3TW, as it had been designated, was destroyed. Nothing could be done at Priory Street to re-start production so after some intensive searching a small disused factory at Warwick was located and such machine tools as could be salvaged from the ruins of Priory Street were transferred and put to work in Warwick. Some of the 3SWs were made but something new was soon evolved for the

forces. This was a 350cc ohv single based on the pre-war 3H and titled the 3HW. One major difference was that the rocker boxes were cast integrally with the cast iron cylinder head in place of the aluminium boxes on the 3H and Tiger 80. Scarce aluminium was needed for projects with a higher priority than motor cycles. By June 1941 machines were coming off the track at Warwick. Meanwhile the management were thinking ahead and a decision had to be made on a new and permanent home for the company. Rebuilding Priory Street had been considered but the city council put a stop to that because it would be too vulnerable in the event of further air raids and because they had plans for re-developing this very important central site. (This came to fruition some years after the war.) So the management looked outside the city, and a green field site at Meriden, four miles from the city centre towards Birmingham, was finally chosen. Despite local objections, Whitehall gave its blessing to the suggestion and building went ahead at a rate which only happens in wartime. Work commenced in July 1941 and by March 1942 some machinery was installed and working. Meriden was a single level factory laid out for motor cycle production, which it did very successfully for many years. Triumph produced 49,700 motor cycles during the war, despite the interruption caused by the bombing. This compares with 30,000 produced for the Great War. Many other products were also made, one of which was a mobile generator for the RAF which employed a 500cc twin cylinder engine based on the Speed Twin.

After the war, Triumph caused something of a stir by dropping all their single cylinder models and announcing an all-twin range. This included the new 350cc 3T de Luxe, the engine of which bore a faint resemblance to the ill-fated 3TW. Then there were the Speed Twin and the Tiger 100. These were basically the same as produced in 1939 but now had Triumph telescopic forks, four gallon fuel tanks and a separate gear-driven dynamo and magneto in place of the Magdyno. It had been the intention to produce a civilian version of the 3HW, the 3H, but nothing came of this as the demand for the twins was so strong. For the first time ever Triumph did not include a side valve machine in the range.

The Triumph Spring Wheel was also introduced at this time. This was a clever scheme of rear suspension incorporated within the hub. To convert a rigid back end to sprung all one had to do was change the wheel. It must be said that movement was very limited but it was better than nothing and was used on two winning Manx Grand Prix machines.

DESTRUCTION COMPLETE. Scenes at the Priory Street factory after the great air raid of 14/15th November 1940. The centre of the city was obliterated. The Triumph factory was right in the centre, only a short step from the ancient cathedral, which was also gutted. The hundred or so night shift workers took to the shelters and amazingly there were no casualties, although elsewhere in the city 554 people died and 865 were seriously injured. The pilot batch of 50 of the new 3TW lightweight motor cycle for the forces was awaiting despatch and was destroyed. No more was heard of this interesting little lightweight although certain features of it reappeared on a new 350 twin in 1946.

3HW IN ACTION. The 3HW was developed into a very useful military motor cycle, one of which is seen here with the author at the helm. It handled well and was reliable, its only weakness being the lack of an air cleaner which in Burma's dust put paid to piston rings in less than 2000 miles.

350cc 3HW MILITARY MODEL. The destruction of the 3TW in the Coventry blitz and the abandonment of the project meant that something else had to be found quickly to replace it. The temporary factory in Warwick had been converted into a machine shop and production of army parts and some 350 side valves put in hand. By June 1941 complete machines were being built. These were 3HWs. This model was derived from the pre-war 3H, hence the title. The engine was a single cylinder of 70 x 89mm (349cc) with rocker boxes cast integrally with the head. The rest of the specification was strictly civilian – 4-speed gearbox, cradle frame, girder forks, 7 inch brakes, 6v electrics and Magdyno. Certain military items were added – panniers, a prop stand like a shooting stick that pivoted from below the saddle, headlamp mask, etc.

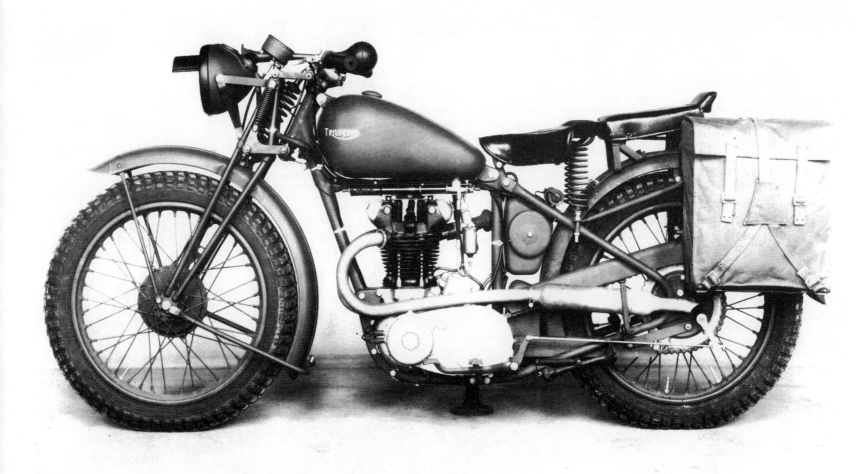

1940 350cc 3TW MILITARY MODEL. This was the Triumph submission to meet the Government specification for a new military motor cycle. BSA, Matchless and Royal Enfield also contributed. The 3TW was a 350cc ohv vertical twin with a 3-speed gearbox built in unit with the engine. It had a rigid frame and girder forks. A unique item was the alternator in the timing chest to supply lighting current. This was the first appearance of an alternator for this purpose on a motor cycle. The specification called for an engine of over 250cc and a maximum weight of 250lb. The 3TW in its original form with aluminium head and barrel weighed 247lb but when aluminium became unobtainable and cast iron replaced it, the weight went up to 260lb.

1942 TRIUMPH GENERATOR SET. This generator set was one of the products made by Triumph during the war in addition to motor cycles. It was made for the Royal Air Force and used for starting aircraft engines, battery charging and supplying current for other purposes. The generator was of BTH manufacture driven by a 500cc twin cylinder fan-cooled engine based on the Speed Twin and governed to run at 5000rpm. It was started by handle, although some had a kickstarter fitted. The head and barrel were alloy and were adapted after the war for use on the Grand Prix model and the 1948 TR5 Trophy. The unusual square shape was necessary to enable the flat cooling cowlings to be fitted closely to the engine. A two-wheeled trailer mounted on motor cycle wheels and tyres was provided to carry the generator. During the war Triumph also made aircraft components, tank track links, steering housings and two-wheeled stretcher carriers.

On to the 1960s

This chapter covers the period when I joined Triumph as Publicity Manager at the end of 1945. It is therefore of great interest to me as I participated in what I shall always regard as the most exciting and successful period of the British motor cycle industry. With Edward Turner firmly in the saddle as Managing Director and his vertical twin on the threshold of its years of phenomenal success, it was definitely the time and place to be around.

Production was the name of the game, and every effort was concentrated on getting the maximum number of motor cycles off the end of the track each week. This was not easy, as the war had only just finished and there were material shortages of all kinds. It took a long time to get into top gear again and I remember a weekly production of 250 machines being regarded with satisfaction whereas, before I finally left Meriden, anything up to 1300 had been known.

The first Isle of Man race after the war was the 1946 Manx Grand Prix and it was won by Ernie Lyons on a Triumph Tiger 100 in appalling weather conditions. A few weeks later, Lyons beat both bikes and cars on the famous Shelsley Walsh climb. It was a works bike but this did not mean that Triumph was going racing. This was left to Norton, AJS and Velocette, who continued to pour large sums of money into the design and development of superb racers, which tended to divert attention from their showroom models, the ones that paid the wages. Triumph, on the other hand, put all their efforts into the showroom models and this soon began to produce results. Demand went sky high and our poor sales staff were almost scared to lift the 'phone when it rang. Bikes had to be allocated to dealers on as fair a basis as possible but most dealers were convinced that their deadly rivals up the road were getting more bikes than them. Our advertising did not extend much further than putting the Triumph logo in the middle of the page and leaving it at that. Jack Welton, a good old stalwart from Bettmann days, controlled the sales office and he had a very difficult job.

The business prospered not only in the UK but also overseas, particularly in America, a market on which Edward Turner himself had been concentrating his attention since before the war. This got so big that in the end the company had two wholly-owned subsidiary companies, one on the east coast and one on the west coast, who divided the USA between them and built up a tremendous volume of business which at times absorbed anything up to 75% of the output.

The model range continued to develop. 1950 saw the 650cc Thunderbird designed to meet the constant demand for more power, particularly from America. It was a fairly simple "bore & stroke" job to produce the 650 engine, and as the rest of the bike was identical to the Speed Twin the extra costs were not high. The customers were happy to pay an additional £10 and it was well worth it. This was profitable for the company and the Thunderbird soon overtook the Speed Twin in the sales race, stimulated no doubt by the demonstration at Montlhéry when three Thunderbirds covered 500 miles each at 90mph. In 1953 the Speed Twin had an alternator, now found on most vehicles and first used on the ill-fated 3TW of 1940. Also in 1953 a single cylinder model reappeared in the range, the 150cc ohv Terrier, quickly followed by the 200cc Tiger Cub, which established a splendid reputation in the hands of both ride-to-work owners and trials riders.

Bonneville Salt Flats in Utah were the scene of a sensational piece of high speed motoring in 1956 when a streamlined shell propelled by a 650cc Triumph engine clocked 214mph. This was not accepted by the F.I.M. but no one took much notice of that fact and rider Allen came with the streamliner to be fêted at the Earls Court Show. This historic machine now has an honoured place in the National Motorcycle Museum near Birmingham. In 1962, Bill Johnson, another American, finally put the record in the book at 224.57mph with a machine similar to Allen's. Two years before this we saw the ultimate 650 and probably the most famous and best loved Triumph of all – the Bonneville 120. The origin of the name is obvious and the "Bonnie" (shades of the "Riccy") established itself as the leader in its field. It was the first production motor cycle to lap the Isle of Man at 100mph, it won the Thruxton 500 Mile race, the Bol d'Or 24 Hour race in France and many others. Two Bonneville engines linked in tandem in a streamlined shell and ridden by Bob Leppan achieved 245.6mph and became the fastest Triumph ever!

Irrespective of all these exciting highlights, the Meriden factory continued to prosper, which was its purpose in life. If its products broke a few records that was fine but it was not the name of the game, which was to make money, and Meriden certainly did this for many years.

In 1964, Edward Turner retired but retained a seat on the BSA board. Three years after this he retired altogether but he did design a 350cc twin for the BSA Group in a freelance capacity. Due to the financial problems which beset the group, it never reached the production stage. Triumph without Turner was never the same and those who came after him were not of the same calibre. He was a giant in the motor cycle industry and not too much notice should be taken of those writers who today try to belittle a man they did not know. His achievements in building up the most successful company in the industry and the motor cycles he produced are sufficient testimony to the man and his character. He died in 1973.

1946 350cc DE LUXE 3T. The original intention had been to announce the 3T, a new 350 twin, in 1939, and the front cover of *The Motor Cycle* dated 8th September, which featured the 3T, had already been printed. War started on 3rd September, the front covers were scrapped, and the 3T had to wait until 1946. The 3TW for the forces was also due out in 1940 but the first batch was destroyed in the Coventry blitz, so there must have been some evil force determined to stop 350 twins at the time. The 1946 3T engine bore some resemblance to the 3TW as it had rocker boxes cast integrally with the head, but that was about all. The specification otherwise was similar to the 500 twins – separate 4-speed gearbox, gear-driven magneto and dynamo, telescopic forks and an instrument panel in the petrol tank.

1946 500cc SPEED TWIN. The
only major postwar change was
the adoption of hydraulically-
damped telescopic forks of
Triumph design and
manufacture. The 4 gallon fuel
tank scheduled for 1940 was also
included. The finish, needless to
say, was the famous Amaranth

Red which had been the hallmark
of the Speed Twin since its
introduction. This popular model,
which made such an impact when
announced, was all set for many
years of popularity. It was fast,
quiet, accelerated very briskly
and, with the new forks, was a lot
more comfortable.

1946 350cc 3H (above) and 1946 350cc TIGER 85 (below). There were two non-starters in the Triumph range for 1946, the single cylinder 3H and the twin cylinder Tiger 85. The 3H was a civilianised black and chrome version of the khaki 3HW and the Tiger 85 was a high performance 3T. That was the intention but nothing came of it, although both were catalogued. Simply put, they were squeezed out of existence by the enormous demand for the 500 twins.

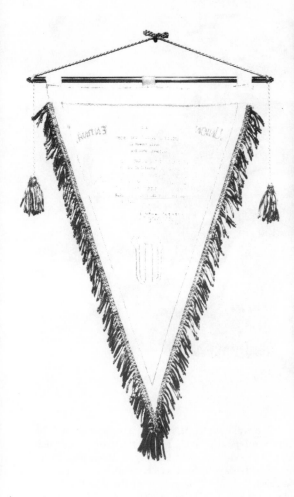

LYONS ON SHELSLEY. Ernie Lyons storming up Shelsley Walsh, 5th October 1946, on his Manx G P-winning Tiger 100. He recorded fastest time of the day for two or four wheels, much to the chagrin of the car racers. To commemorate his win, the Union of Argentine Motorcyclists sent Triumph a beautiful embroidered banner. What became of it, history does not relate, but there is a photograph.

500 TRIALS SPECIAL. Always keen supporters of trials, Triumph had a problem in 1946. The range was all twins and the popular theory was that you had to have the 'thump' of a single cylinder to get any grip. We toyed with the idea of using a 3HW, suitably modified, but decided against it as a retrograde step. Finally Jim Alves tweaked a 350 twin into shape, practised throttle control and won the Cotswold Cups Trial first time out. Then the 500 was looked at and this one, with what looks like an ex-generator set head, was one result. It was generally reckoned that the 350 was easier to handle, so the bigger twins took to scrambling in the hands of Johnny Giles, Ken Heanes and others, and were very successful.

ALLAN JEFFERIES. Allan was one of the greatest all-rounders this country has ever produced. Speedway, one-day trials, six-day trials, scrambles, road racing – Allan tried them all and was usually very successful. This picture shows him pressing on to finish second in the Senior Clubmans TT in the Isle of Man in June 1947. He averaged 75.23mph on a more or less standard Tiger 100. In 1948, Triumph gained the only Team Prize won by a British manufacturer in the International Six Days Trial. Jefferies, Alves and Gaymer were the riders. Allan Jefferies also captained the British Trophy Team that won the trial that year. A year later he was at Montlhéry riding in the 500-miles-at-90mph Thunderbird demonstration. Yes – a real all-rounder!

1948 SENIOR TT GRAND PRIX MODEL. In a fit of misguided enthusiasm, Triumph became involved in the 1948 Senior TT through the efforts of Nigel Spring, who had transferred his attention from Nortons to the GP Triumph. He had top rank riders – Freddie Frith, Ken Bills and Bob Foster – and there were other very competent performers on the GP like Vic Willoughby, Albert Moule and Syd Barnett. But they all retired with various problems and Triumph reverted once more to its normal state of sanity. The model above was ridden by Ken Bills and was fairly standard apart from the nearside oil filler.

350cc TRIALS PROTOTYPE. Ridden by Bob Manns in the 1948 season, this 350 looks reasonably standard apart from the alloy cylinder head. At first glance this might have come from the early wartime 3TW but it has the square fins, straight ports and fixing bosses of a generator set, so it may have come from one, scaled down to fit the 350 barrel. The Competition Department were very good at building "one offs" like this – as long as the Managing Director did not know anything about it!

1949 500cc TR5 TROPHY. The Triumph team in the 1948 ISDT was the only British manufacturer's team to win a Team Prize. They used specially-built Speed Twins with alloy heads and barrels but the machines were far from ideal for the job. Something lighter and easier to handle was needed, and after much experimentation the TR5 Trophy was born. With two inches off the Speed Twin wheelbase, alloy head and barrel as per the GP, a narrow 2½ gallon tank, two-into-one exhaust and alloy guards, something like 60lb dry weight was saved. The result was one of the most pleasing and effective Triumph models ever. Today, an example in good condition will command a very high price indeed. When first announced £195.11.8d. could have bought one.

1948 3T AA BOX SIDECAR. It seems a little harsh to harness an inoffensive 350 like the 3T to an AA box sidecar full of car repair gear. There is no record of any quantity of outfits like this being supplied. The usual tow horse employed by the AA was the Speed Twin, of which quite a few were delivered in 1948.

1949 500cc 5/3W MILITARY MODEL. Following the 3TW disaster Triumph built a 500 side valve to meet a Ministry requirement for a 500 twin not exceeding 300lb in weight. The war finished, the project disappeared and Triumph put the engine into a machine using as many stock parts as possible, including the Trophy frame, 4-speed gearbox, tele forks and nacelle headlamp. It was called the "Hybrid" but was the forerunner of the successful TRW, which sold to overseas forces in fair numbers, although sales in the UK were limited.

THE WHITE HELMETS. The motor cycle display team of the Royal Corps of Signals, official title "The White Helmets", has been in existence since the early 1920s. In those days, horses were used as well as motor cycles because the horse was just as much a part of the army's equipment. The remarkable thing is that right from the start the team has used Triumph almost exclusively. Looking at old photographs one recognises the trusty side valves giving good service. Since the last war, most current types of Triumph have been pressed into use at one time or another.

MONTLHÉRY THUNDERBIRDS. The Thunderbird demonstration at Montlhéry in September 1949 has been described so many times that it is not necessary to go into any detail here except to say that the aim of covering 500 miles at 90mph with three machines was totally successful. Here we see the three machines after being ridden back from Montlhéry (as well as being ridden there), with Alex Scobie being interviewed by David Martin of the BBC. Len Bayliss is on No 3 and Bob Manns No 2. Other riders involved were Allan Jefferies and Jim Alves. The character on the right is the author.

1950 650cc THUNDERBIRD. Like the Speed Twin which set a world-wide fashion for 500cc vertical twins, the Thunderbird, introduced in 1949, led the way to bigger vertical twins, 650s, 700s, 750s, 800s and even 900s. It was Edward Turner's opinion that 650cc was the limit for vertical twins and, from the stories that get around about vibration on bigger twins, he was probably right. The Thunderbird was identical to the Speed Twin apart from the extra 150cc and a change of colour, but the customer got his money's worth (£10 extra) as the performance was appreciably better than the 500's.

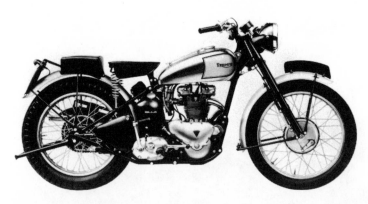

1951 500cc TR5 TROPHY. A major change in this model was the die cast head and barrel, with the elegant close-pitched finning which replaced the previous square components descended from the wartime generator set. The Tiger 100 was similarly equipped but in this case the alloy units replaced cast iron, a very considerable improvement. This must be one of the best looking Triumph engines ever produced, the slim, closely set fins being particularly attractive.

1951 500cc TIGER 100. The Tiger 100 retained its popularity for many years as a really fast and easily handled tourer which could more than hold its own against comparable models of other makes. Owners could buy a kit of high performance parts which, of properly put together, would provide performance on a par with the Grand Prix. In 1951 the cast iron head and barrel were changed for die cast alloy components with attractive close-pitched finning. In standard trim with 7.6:1 pistons the engine produced 32bhp at 6500rpm and with a dry weight of only 355lb the reason for the performance is obvious.

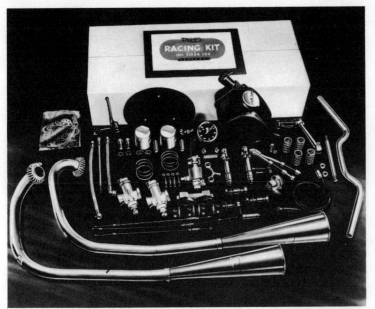

RACING TIGER 100. Any owner wishing to go racing with his Tiger 100 in the 1950s could buy a very comprehensive kit of high performance parts. Then, if he knew what he was doing, he would finish up with a machine that would really go. The kit comprised pistons (choice of compression ratios) two racing camshafts, valve springs, two carburettors, dual throttle cables, petrol pipes, tachometer, one gallon oil tank, exhaust pipes with megaphones, folding footrest, racing type handlebar, racing number plate, short brake rod, folding kickstarter, washers and gaskets. The two photographs show the kit and a Tiger 100 fitted with it.

TIGER 100 FOR DAYTONA.
Following the win in 1948, there were always plenty of Triumphs in the Daytona Races in the 1950s. Tigers were the popular choice and a few were even prepared at the works following pressure from the States, which was rapidly building up into our most important market. The Americans were very enthusiastic about racing as a sales aid and even Edward Turner had to give way occasionally. The Tiger 100 above was prepared for Ed Kretz Snr, the legendary American ace. It featured twin carburettors, remote float bowl, rear set rests with brake and gear lever to suit, large oil tank, and rear Spring Wheel – no great departures from standard.

PETER HAMMOND, 1953 ISDT.
Peter was one of the regulars in the works trials team, along with Jim Alves, Allan Jefferies, Bert Gaymer, Johnny Giles and others from time to time. He did well in the ISDT, where Triumph won manufacturers team prizes with almost monotonous regularity. In this picture he is seen blasting up a hill in the 1953 event held in Gottwaldov, in Czechoslovakia. When his riding days ended Peter concentrated his attentions on a successful motor cycle business in Cirencester.

1953 150cc TERRIER. The Terrier fulfilled an urgent requirement for Triumph to get back into the lightweight field. A youngster buying his first motor cycle, a lightweight, would tend to go for the same make when he wanted something larger. There was a lot of competition and Turner's aim was not to compete on price but to offer a more sophisticated motor cycle, even if it did cost a little more. The Terrier was a four-stroke, it looked like a Triumph with its headlamp nacelle, it had a 4-speed gearbox, decent size brakes, and was finished in the famous Speed Twin red.

1953 500cc ISDT TROPHY. 1948 saw the start of Triumph involvement in the International Six Days Trial and this brought about the birth of the very popular Trophy models in 500cc and, later, 650cc forms (TR5 and TR6). The Triumph team were particularly successful at this time and won a manufacturers team award four years in succession, 1948-51. For a whole team to compete four years running without losing a single mark was some achievement. The machines were meticulously prepared at the works and development was dictated by experience. At all costs the machine had to keep going and duplicate controls and cables, quickly detachable wheels, and seasoned riders who could change a tube in minutes all contributed to this end.

ADVERTISING WITH A LAUGH. High pressure selling ads would have been counter-productive for Triumph after the war, such was the demand for the product. So we gave them a laugh with the series by Alex Oxley on the theme "It's Easy on a Triumph".

JACK WICKEN. Caps with peaks at the back were not regular wear with works riders, but they were practical – they didn't blow off! Here we see Jack Wicken feeding his 500 twin through a sticky section in the 1954 Hurst Cup Trial.

1954 500cc CLASS C RACER. A strictly functional motor cycle this! It was built at the works for American Class C flat track racing, which bears only a very remote resemblance to British speedway, the major difference being that American tracks can be up to a mile long and speeds of 100mph are not uncommon. It is sensational to watch. The engine is a hot Tiger 100 with twin carbs. There is no front brake but the one at the rear appears to be standard.

JIM ALVES. With *his* peak firmly at the front, Jim Alves cracks along on his Terrier in the 1954 Cotswold Cups Trial. A few years earlier he had caused a stir in the trials world by winning this event first time out on a 350 twin.

KEEP GOING FOR A GOLD! Rider aiming to be selected for the British teams in the International Six Days Trial had to prove in preliminary tests that they could keep going, come what may. Changing a tube in minutes, or tracing some obscure electrical fault in pouring rain with a mud-covered bike had to be done, and done quickly, if they were to make the short list. Prior to the event every item on the bike is checked and double checked and here the Lucas expert is sorting out a wiring problem whilst Trophy Team member Alves watches intently. In the trial, outside assistance is absolutely forbidden but it has been known for a team manager or mechanic to make sotto voce suggestions from a respectable distance!

1956 ISDT 650. In 1955 the Trophy model acquired some real rear suspension, which must have been a great relief to ISDT riders blasting over rough mountain tracks. This 1956 actual works model illustrates the lengths to which the factory went to ensure a troublefree ride. Nail catchers, duplicated cables, spare spokes, rubber-covered headlamp, two-into-one exhaust, QD wheels, crankcase shield, map case on the tank – and, of course, only to be ridden by the best riders in the business.

SHOW BUSINESS. The annual show at Earls Court was an event that generated a lot of activity in my department and the works. The exhibits were all plated and polished to a very high degree, far in excess of the standard seen in the dealer's showroom, good though that was. The design of the stand was studied very closely by Edward Turner and I had to choose very carefully the contractor who was going to build it. It cost a lot of money and it was essential that it should exceed the efforts of our competitors at BSA, Norton, Matchless and Royal Enfield – which I like to think it usually did. This "Big T" design, ablaze with lights, was seen at the 1956 Show.

1956 TIGER 100R FOR USA. Our American companies were very race orientated and even Edward Turner was obliged to give way on occasions to their demands to supply something competitive. This Tiger 100 was sent to the Triumph Corporation of Baltimore in December 1956. They probably wanted it for Daytona the following March, but no positive information is available.

1960 350cc TWENTY ONE. The Twenty-One was so called because it was introduced in 1957, which was the 21st anniversary of the Triumph Engineering Co. Ltd. Another reason given was that 350cc in America equates to 21 cubic inches. Whatever the reason, the Twenty-one was certainly a departure from previous Triumph practice. The engine was a vertical twin, but the gearbox was built in unit, a practice that was extended to the larger engines some years later. Semi rear enclosure was another feature plus a very adequate front guard to promote cleaner, drier riding. The prototype testing of this model was longer, harder and faster than was usual and this paid off later when production models proved to be particularly trouble-free.

BILL MARTIN – CUB EXTRAORDINARY. At Bonneville Utah in August 1959, Bill Martin, a Burbank, California Triumph dealer riding a 200cc Tiger Cub-powered streamliner, set a new AMA two-way record of 139.82mph over a measured mile. A one-way speed of 149.135mph was achieved. The T20's engine reached 9100rpm during the record runs. The engine used stock ignition, camshaft, piston and valves. The inlet port was cleaned out and the rocker arms lightened. JOMO outer valve springs and Webco alloy pushrods were used. Carburation was looked after by a 1 7/32 inch Amal carburettor. Bill Martin at that time was 49 years of age and a former racing car driver. Preparation and tuning of the engine was done by his two sons, seen here with their father and the streamliner. Quite a performance for a Cub!

BILL MARTIN'S 150mph TIGER CUB. Head-on view of the 200cc streamliner with Martin alongside.

DALE MARTIN. Bill Martin's eldest son on his own T20S, which he used for record attempts at Bonneville in 1959.

1959 BONNEVILLE 120. The Bonneville was the ultimate high performance Triumph twin. It was the final step in a long chain of development dating back some years. Tiger 100 owners could get near racing performance with a kit of special parts, but this was not enough. The short answer was more ccs or "more cubes" as the Americans were wont to put it. The result was the 650 Thunderbird and the Tiger 110.

Then the game started all over again, to make the T110 quicker. In the end the factory put it all together and the result was the Bonneville, a twin carb 650 producing 46bhp in standard trim (12bhp more than the first Thunderbird). The first "Bonnie" (as it soon came to be called) had a nacelle headlamp, but this was soon dropped in favour of a separate lamp and a more sporting appearance.

1959 500cc SPEED TWIN. In 1957 a new 350, the Twenty-one, was announced with unit-construction engine/gearbox and semi-enclosure of the rear end. Two years later what was virtually the same machine appeared but with a 500cc engine. This replaced the existing Speed Twin. The engine was oversquare, 69 x 65.5mm (490cc) with a 7:1 compression ratio, and produced 27bhp at 6500rpm. The same semi-enclosure of the rear end was retained but the finish was the traditional Speed Twin amaranth red. It continued in this form until 1964 when the rear enclosure was reduced to a minimum.

JOHNNY GILES. Triumph were among the first to exploit the use of lightweights in trials, a practice which has now become so universal that events are held today, restricted to "big bangers" just for fun! Here we see Johnny Giles, Triumph works rider, "flat in second" through the mud on his Tiger Cub. The Cub did very well for a time and even scored a win in the arduous Scottish Six Days Trial.

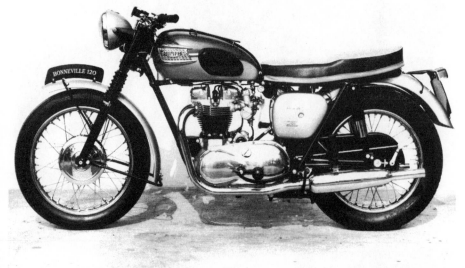

1960 650cc BONNEVILLE 120. This was the model that made the enthusiast's heart beat a little faster. It had a twin cylinder pushrod ohv engine of 71 x 82mm (649cc), with a compression ratio of 8.5:1, developing 46bhp at 6500rpm, twin carburettors (no aircleaners), 4-speed gearbox (ratios 4.66, 5.55, 7.88 and 11.38:1), and 8 inch front, 7 inch rear brakes. Wheelbase was 54½ inches, weight 393lb. Price in 1960 was £284.13.6d. In 1969 Malcolm Uphill riding a Bonneville won the Production TT in the Isle of Man at 99.99mph with a record lap at 100.37mph, the first time a production machine had lapped the Island at 100mph.

1960 650cc TROPHY (TR6). Very similar to the Bonneville in general specification but with a single carburettor, 8:1 cr engine developing 40bhp at 6500rpm. This model quickly built up a formidable record of success in competition, particularly in the USA, where the Jack Pine Enduro, Catalina Grand Prix, Big Bear Run (four years in succession) and most other big American classics were dominated by the TR6. The first Trophy models in the fifties were developed for the International Six Day Trial and this type of event was always a happy hunting ground for the model, either as a 500 (TR5) or 650 (TR6).

1960 200cc TIGER CUB. The popularity of the Tiger Cub was never in doubt from the moment it was launched. It was a refreshing four-stroke change from all the two-strokes on the market. It went well, handled superbly and was economical. The 1960 T20 sported some partial enclosure at the rear which was not unattractive. The specification details were much as before – 63 x 64mm, 199cc pushrod ohv engine developing 10bhp at 6000rpm, Zenith carburettor, 4-speed unit gearbox (ratios 7.2, 9.4, 14.4 and 21.6:1), weight 205 lb. Price £155.15s.

1961 200cc TIGER CUB T20 S/L. This was the Tiger Cub Sports model and was offered in two versions, the T20 S/L high performance model and the T20T with lower compression for trials work. The S/L had a 9:1 compression ratio and developed 14.5bhp at 6500rpm. Gear ratios were 7.13, 8.56, 13.37 and 19.8:1. It was fast and handled particularly well, its light weight of just 210lb being a contributing factor. Price £164.1.0d.

1961 650cc TIGER 110. The 110 was really the touring version of the Bonneville and was often reckoned, by those who claimed to know, to be the best bike Triumph ever made and the most enjoyable to ride. It was similar in most respects to the Bonneville but the engine had one carburettor instead of two and produced 40bhp compared to the Bonneville's 46. It also had the rear enclosure adopted for the less sporting models of the range.

JUST FOR PUBLICITY. We used to stage a number of shots like this every year. They came in useful to fill dull corners in the catalogue and showed off the bikes in natural surroundings. The lad was one of our testers and the two girls were from the office, the one on the left being Olivia, the author's secretary. Cheaper than paying for models!

THE MASTER RIDES AGAIN! A stock joke among motor cyclists is that manufacturers never ride their own products, the inference being that if they did they would design them differently! This was certainly untrue at Triumph where in the postwar years most members of the senior management could be seen on two wheels. Some, like Service Manager Alec Masters or Sales Manager Neale Shilton – or even the Publicity Manager (!) – could be seen riding to work every day, wet or fine. The photograph shows the boss, Edward Turner, and the author. The occasion was a publicity gallop round the Shropshire Hills for the benefit of the press.

TRIUMPH IN FIJI. Fiji is a long way from Meriden but the police authorities there knew where to come for the best motor cycles. How pleasant to be able to ride around in shirt sleeve order, but the fairing on the Speed Twin suggests that it is not always dry and sunny, even in Fiji.

SERVING THE POLICE. Right from the days of the first Speed Twin in 1938 the police came to Triumph for their motor cycles and in postwar years Triumph completely dominated the market. A similar situation existed in many overseas markets. First the Speed Twin, then the Thunderbird were the favoured models and eventually a very specialised Thunderbird was developed which became known as "The Saint". Escort duties always fall to police motor cyclists whether the escort is of a ship's boiler or, as in this case, General Eisenhower, President of the United States, accompanied by Prime Minister Macmillan. Speeds were usually low with frequent stops, which posed problems for clutches and engine temperatures.

SCOOTERS? The Triumph high performance image seems far removed from the world of scooters, but scooters there were, bearing the world famous logo. Firstly, in 1958 there was the Tigress (above), designed by Edward Turner and made by BSA in two versions, 250cc ohv twin and 175cc two-stroke. This was quite a luxurious little vehicle but did not make much impact on a market that was already fading. The second one, also a Turner creation, started as the Tina in 1962 and had automatic transmission by belt with expanding and contracting pulleys. The engine was a 100cc two-stroke. The T10 of 1965 (right) was an updated version with the teething troubles cured (well, most of them). When everything was right it worked well but there were problems exacerbated by novice customers. Nevertheless it lasted until the late 1960s. The girl in the striped shirt is Mollie Peters, one of the Bond lovelies from the film *Thunderball*.

1962 650cc THUNDERBIRD (6T). Apart from the pistons still going up and down together, there is not much resemblance between this model and the original 1950 Thunderbird. This version has alloy head, massive finning, unit-construction gearbox, siamesed exhaust, twin tube frame with pivoted fork rear suspension, full-width front hub, partial rear enclosure – but there is one familiar item, the headlamp nacelle is still the same. A truly handsome motor cycle and one that performed in the best Thunderbird tradition.

AMERICAN TIGER 100. The Americans are a great sporting race and they enter into motor cycle competitions with their usual fervour. The events they organise are many and varied. Road racing, cross country, enduros, flat track, even the ISDT, which was held in the USA in 1971. The demands on manufacturers are heavy to supply bikes for all these things and Triumph, while sympathetic, was not over-keen to produce "specials" which did not come down the track like the others, in a well ordered manner. This very businesslike Tiger 100 was supplied to Johnson Motors, the West Coast distributors, in 1964.

TRIUMPH ACES. In the 1950s and 1960s the Triumph record in long distance events was unparalleled. Triumph works riders invariably found themselves selected for the British national teams in these events, particularly the International Six Days Trial. Here we see the Triumph team in the Welsh Three Day Trial of 1962, an eliminating event for the "big one". From left to right Roy Peplow, Gordon Blakeway, John Giles and Ken Heanes. The bikes were assorted 500s and 650s.

RECORD BREAKER AT
MERIDEN. In September 1962
American Bill Johnson piloted a
Bonneville-powered streamliner
to a new World's Speed Record of
224.57mph. The machine was
subsequently flown to England
for display at the Earls Court
Show. It is here seen outside the
Triumph works at Meriden with
the intrepid "driver" chatting to
workers with Edward Turner
looking on. The streamliner was
17ft in length, 20in wide, had a
wheelbase of 96 inches and
weighed 400lb. There was no
suspension and the front wheel
incorporated hub centre steering
using a Triumph rear Spring
Wheel hub shell. The driver sat in
the centre with a vertical column
between his knees at the top of
which the handlebars were
pivoted. A front brake lever was
used to operate the throttle
instead of a twistgrip. The engine
and gearbox were behind the
driver and the positive stop
gearchange lever was mounted
on the side of the cockpit by the
driver's right hand. With a
compression ratio of 11:1 the
engine was fed alcohol vapour
from two large Amal carburettors.
A drum brake was fitted to the
rear wheel, operated by a central
pedal.

FASTEST TRIUMPH EVER! In August 1966 Bob Leppan in his Gyronaut X-1, powered by two Triumph 650cc engines, recorded a two way average over the mile of 245.6mph. This American record could not be recognised in Europe as at that time the F.I.M. engine capacity limit was 1000cc. Bob Leppan and his engineer Joe Bruflodt who were Triumph dealers in a big way in Detroit later installed two three-cylinder Trident engines in Gyronaut X-1, but the front suspension collapsed at around 270mph and Leppan was seriously injured, though happily he recovered.

THE TRIUMPH OWNERS MOTORCYCLE CLUB. Founded in the 1950s, this club is large and flourishing, with branches all over the UK and several overseas. Here we see a group of members on a visit to the National Motorcycle Museum near Birmingham, where they were able to inspect a wide selection of immaculate Triumphs of all ages – as well as other makes of course!

MERIDEN WORKS 1949. An aerial photograph of the Triumph works at Meriden, near Coventry. Although taken in 1949, it is still virtually as built in 1942. Later it was extended in all directions. The two-storey block at the right-hand corner housed the administrative and accounts departments on the ground floor and the drawing office, including Edward Turner's office, on the first floor. The assembly and despatch areas were in the front left corner (behind the row of cars) and the remainder comprised machine shops, paint and plating, heat treatment, frame shop and all the rest. The long low building sticking out on the left was the works canteen. Meriden had a pleasant rural aspect and was a good place to work in. Sadly it is no more.

a

b

c

d

MERIDEN IN THE 1960s. a) 500cc Assembly. b) Same place with Director and Designer Bert Hopwood inspecting his handiwork at close quarters.
c) The rolling road test rig which superseded the human tester.
d) 650cc engine assembly track.

MERIDEN, THE END. After the ill-fated co-operative had collapsed, the factory was sold and "developers" moved in. Demolition was swift and by mid-1984 this famous factory, producer of one of the world's great motor cycles, was a heap of rubble and twisted girders. Today the site is a housing estate. I often wonder if the new residents living on this historic piece of ground are ever disturbed in their sleep by the harsh roar of a ghostly Bonneville engine flat out on the brake?

As a parting shot I quote from the Introduction to the 1908 Triumph catalogue: "We are still convinced ... that the scientifically constructed single-cylinder engine of sufficient power and flexibility is much more preferable for touring purposes than the twin-cylinder. It is infinitely simpler in construction, freer from trouble, and more easily handled and understood by the average rider."

So much for your Speed Twins, Thunderbirds and Bonnevilles!

General Index

Model Index